Written by Bernard Planche
Illustrated by Christian Broutin

173653

Specialist adviser: Dr John Mack,
African Curator,
The Museum of Mankind, London

ISBN 1 85103 014 X
First published 1986 in the United Kingdom by
Moonlight Publishing Ltd,
131 Kensington Church Street, London W8

P O C K E T • W O R L D S

Living on a Tropical Island

Where fish and fruit are plentiful,
and the sea is warm and clear...

Did you know that there are wonderful islands of palm trees and soft sand, set in a warm, clear sea? **They are tropical islands.**

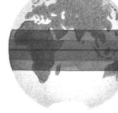

The tropics lie where we have marked this orange band on the map.

The islands are like gardens, full of flowers and delicious fruit. Under the sea is like a garden too; there is coral of every colour, and shells, and fish darting in and out!

To show you what they are like, we have chosen one island, called Nossy-Be. It lies to the north-west of Madagascar, off the coast of Africa. In the Malagasi language Nossy-Be simply means 'big island'.

Tropical islands often began as volcanoes, bursting up from the bottom of the sea millions of years ago.

The houses are built of leaves.

Each family builds its own house. The
walls are made of bamboo canes and
banana leaves. The roof is covered with
coconut palms. So that floodwater cannot
get into the houses in stormy weather,
they are built on little platforms to raise
them above ground-level.

The houses have just one room. People only use their houses at night, when they go to bed on mats made of woven raffia. There is no running water, but if you want a bath, the sea is close by! Or if you prefer, you could have a shower under a waterfall.

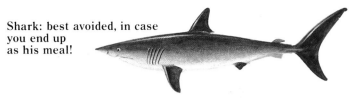

Shark: best avoided, in case you end up as his meal!

Nearly everybody in these islands lives by fishing, there are so many delicious fish swimming in the waters around Nossy-Be! Each fisherman makes his own canoe. He finds a hardwood tree and cuts it down. Then he hollows it out with a small axe. To make the canoe more stable, he puts on a frame called an outrigger which balances it as it floats. The sail is a square of cotton.

Ray

Grouper

Canoe-racing

On feast days, the young men race each other. The whole village lines up on the beach to watch!

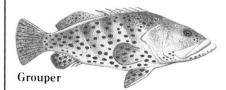

Barracuda

Fishing

As soon as the sun is up, fishermen lay baskets rather like lobster-pots on the sea-bottom. By nightfall they will be full of little fish. Then the men pay out a net from the back of their canoes as they paddle towards the shore. When they draw in the net it is crammed with strange-sounding fish: thread-fin, barracuda, tiger-fish, parrot-fish. In no time at all they will all have been eaten, grilled or raw, soaked in coconut milk.

The fish are attached to poles to carry them up to the houses.

Children swimming where it is safe from sharks can see all sorts of amazing fish, the kind that you see in an aquarium! Coral, growing like flowers under the sea, is made by tiny animals. They have formed a reef, which shelters groupers (1),

zebra-fish (2), butterfly-fish (3),
Moorish-idols (4) and surgeon-fish (5).
Watch out for the sea-urchin spines (6),
anemones (7) which sting, scorpion-fish
(8) which are poisonous, and the
sharp-toothed moray eels (9)!

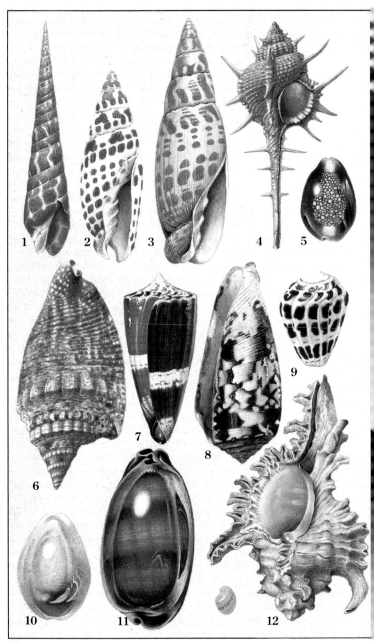

The sun rises quickly in the tropics.

On Sunday mornings the children rush down to the beach as soon as they can. They make rafts out of coconuts. After having a swim, they lie in the shade of the coconut palms, making necklaces out of shells, or using the shells as counters in their games.

Do you like collecting shells?

Here, at low tide, you might find the shell of a giant clam. When the clams are under the sea, their lips are a phosphorescent blue!

There are hundreds of kinds of shells:
1 2 3: cones; 4 12: murex;
5 10 11: clams; 6 7 8 9: cowries.

This boy has already got a murex and now he's found a giant clam!

Climbing for coconuts

Children climb the coconut palms using steps which have been cut into the trunk. You have to be as agile as a monkey to get to the top! Halfway up a metal collar has been fixed round the trunk to stop the rats and mice climbing up and eating the coconuts.

Every bit of a coconut is useful.

The clear 'milk' is like fresh water; the white flesh can be eaten by itself or used for making cakes, oil, candles, even soap – it's coconut oil which makes your soap go frothy. The hairy outside part is used to make mats, and the hard shell makes good bowls!

Here are some tropical fruits, but there are lots of others!

1 Plantain 2 Banana 3 Pineapple 4 Mango 5 Pawpaw

In the middle of the island are huge fields of
sugar. Here the canes are beginning to grow.

The stalk of the cane is full of sweet juice.
Children pick the canes and suck them.

When the canes are two metres high, they
come into bloom, with flowers like feathers.

Before the harvest, the dead leaves are set on fire. The smoke smells of toffee!

The sugar canes are cut by hand, and then taken to the factory on a little steam-train.

At the factory, the canes are pressed. The juice crystallises into brown sugar.

Cooking is usually done out of doors. As well as fish cooked over open fires, there are lots of vegetables, salads and rice.

Yams are eaten mashed or fried.

Manioc roots are grated and pressed.

Maniocs and yams grow underground like potatoes.

The leaves of maniocs can be eaten as well, they taste like spinach. There are even vegetables which grow under the sea: seaweeds. They are full of vitamins and taste a bit like beans.

Turmeric root

Turmeric, another root vegetable, has rather a strong taste. It is powdered and used for flavouring food.

Powdered turmeric is yellow.

Sugar and spice
and all things nice...

Spices taste very strong. Just a little gives a nice flavour to food. The strongest spices are red or green chillies. If you're not used to them, they make your mouth feel as if it's on fire!

Vanilla is a precious spice.

The plant has a beautiful yellow flower. The fruit hangs in bunches of green pods, which grow dark and sweet-smelling as they dry.

Market day

The farmers and fishermen set up their stalls. There are all sorts of bananas: tiny ones, big purple ones that need cooking, and the kind that you know too. Here, ripened by the sun, they smell even more delicious! And then there are the spices: sticks of cinnamon – the bark of a special tree – tied up in bundles, piles of chillies and pepper... Further along there is the fish market: most of the fish will have been caught the night before. Some is dried and smoked. Everything is there to be bargained for – it's all part of the fun of shopping...

Zebus have a hump which stores fat. You see these cow-like animals wandering all over the island. Their meat is very tender.

Animals which survive from prehistoric times. In the forest live lemurs, distant cousins of the monkey. The **macaco** lemur has thick silky fur and huge, wide-open orange eyes to help it see in the dark – it comes out mainly at night. The male is black, the female has red fur. They love eating bananas and mangoes, which they pick with their long fingers. During the day they doze in the sun. They are so friendly they'll come and eat out of your hand! The **chameleon** is an odd creature: it changes colour to hide itself. If it sits on a leaf, it'll go green, but when it moves to a branch it turns brown.

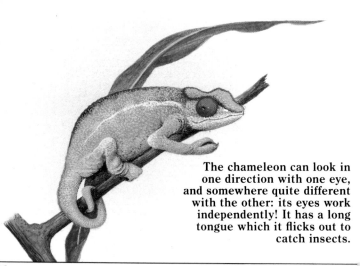

The chameleon can look in one direction with one eye, and somewhere quite different with the other: its eyes work independently! It has a long tongue which it flicks out to catch insects.

Turtles only come on land to lay their eggs.

You can see the females climbing up the beach in the evenings. In the sea they move easily, but on land they have to drag themselves along. The female climbs up above the tide line and digs a hole where she lays up to a hundred eggs. Then she covers them over with sand. The sun warms the nest, and about two months later the baby turtles hatch out and rush down the beach to the sea.

But there are dangers all around.

Birds and fish are waiting to gobble them up! Only a few will survive...

The lakes in the middle of the islands are full of crocodiles. Which make doing your washing there rather exciting!

Rubber-plants, philodendrons, avocadoes – all these plants grow freely here, and much bigger than we see them growing in flower pots at home. On holidays, children pick armfuls of beautiful flowers – they make them into wreaths, or put them in their hair, and round the plates of party food.

1. Hibiscus
2. Bougainvillaea
3. Frangipani
4. Canna lily

Every year, between December and February, cyclones may sweep across the islands. Cyclones are very violent storms. The wind rushes round, spinning in a circle, at 200 kilometres an hour! It whips up the waves until they are higher than houses. Crops are wiped out, trees uprooted, houses swept away... But luckily, after two or three days, the weather settles down, the sun begins to shine again, and the islanders can set about rebuilding their villages and replanting their crops.

An island of sweet smells

The ylang-ylang is a plant grown for its scented flowers. In the daytime the flowers are green.

They open during the night, and in the morning, covered in dew, they turn a lovely lemon-yellow, and have a beautiful scent. These flowers provide a liquid which is the basis for every **perfume** in the world! It takes a hundred kilos of flowers to make a single drop of perfume!

In the wild, the ylang-ylang grows very tall. To make the flowers easier to harvest, people tie the branches down so that they grow sideways along the ground. It makes the trees look very strange!

What is that bird perched on a branch? It's called a toulou. There are lots of other birds on the island – parrots, red cardinals... At mating time cardinals have bright red feathers, so that the island is speckled with brilliant scarlet dots.

Index

Now find out about

other 'Human World' titles available
in the **Pocket Worlds** series